Grief & Loss. Will the pain ever end?

Handbook of proven tools to overcome grief and start living again

☐ **Copyright 2017 by Janet Lee- All rights reserved.**

This document is geared towards providing exact and reliable information in regards to the topic and issue covered. The publication is sold with the idea that the publisher is not required to render accounting, officially permitted, or otherwise, qualified services. If advice is necessary, legal or professional, a practiced individual in the profession should be ordered.

- From a Declaration of Principles which was accepted and approved equally by a Committee of the American Bar Association and a Committee of Publishers and Associations.

In no way is it legal to reproduce, duplicate, or transmit any part of this document in either electronic means or in printed format. Recording of this publication is strictly prohibited and any storage of this document is not allowed unless with written permission from the publisher. All rights reserved.

The information provided herein is stated to be truthful and consistent, in that any liability, in terms of inattention or otherwise, by any usage or abuse of any policies, processes, or directions contained within is the solitary and utter responsibility of the recipient reader. Under no circumstances will any legal responsibility or blame be held against the publisher for any reparation, damages, or monetary loss due to the information herein, either directly or indirectly.

Respective authors own all copyrights not held by the publisher.

The information herein is offered for informational purposes solely, and is universal as so. The presentation of the information is without contract or any type of guarantee assurance.

The trademarks that are used are without any consent, and the publication of the trademark is without permission or backing by the trademark owner. All trademarks and brands within this book are for clarifying purposes only and are the owned by the owners themselves, not affiliated with this document.

Contents

Introduction 5
Chapter 1 – Understanding Grief And Bereavement 7
Chapter 2 – The Symptoms Of Grief 9
Chapter 3 – The Different Stages Of Grief 12
Chapter 4 – Strategies For Coping 18
Chapter 5 – What Happens If There Is No Improvement? 26
Chapter 6 – Helping Someone Else Who Is Grieving .. 29
Conclusion 34

Introduction

Whether you are a grieving individual, wish to help someone who is grieving or a professional working with the grieving I want to thank you for buying the book, "Grief & Loss: Will the pain ever end".

Losing a loved one is arguably one of the most difficult and distressing experiences that any of us will ever experience in our lifetime. Yet in our everyday life we talk about death very little, perhaps because we do not experience it very often compared to our ancestors where the life expectancy was lower and where death was a more common occurrence. For us, due to advances in medicine, these losses typically occur much later in life so we have no "framework" to fall back on and feel lost as to how we should react. In spite of the lack of life experience, we have to one day cope when we are finally confronted with a loss.

Whether the loss is that of a spouse or partner, a family member, a close friend or colleague, a pet or even the loss of a long-term job the process of grieving will have similar emotional, physical, social and spiritual responses to varying degrees. No one person will experience the pain in the same way or to the same intensity but it seems that our society has an acute lack of services to support those who are grieving, to help them through the difficult journey so that they can heal the wounds, rebuild their life and come to terms with their loss.

This practical handbook attempts to make the journey of grieving a little easier for all those who are suffering the loss of a loved one or who would like to support someone they care about get through the pain quicker. We look at the impact of grief on the emotional, physical, social and spiritual state of the individual and how these responses manifest themselves within the 5 stages of the 'grief' model. Finally we give you effective and proven strategies to help you to come to terms with the loss and start to rebuild your life so that you can once again engage in enjoyable and satisfying relationships and pursuits.

Chapter 1 – Understanding Grief And Bereavement

Grief is a natural, involuntary reaction to loss of any kind. It is the emotional response a person feels when they lose someone or something that is of great significance to them. Any loss can give rise to grieving and the more significant the loss the greater the intensity of the grief. The loss can range from arguably the most significant event – the loss of a loved one – to other events such as a marriage breakup, loss of a job, retirement, loss of health or death of a treasured pet. Irrespective of what the loss was, if it was important to you then you will feel a sense of grief and that is completely normal.

Bereavement is the time we spend in grieving and mourning the loss. It is important to know that there is no fixed timetable for how long this may take, for some it may be a matter of weeks or months and for others it may be a year or more. Mourning is an important part of bereavement and you cannot rush it. If you have lost a loved one then attending a funeral will be extremely stressful but it allows us to say goodbye and affirm the reality of what has happened. As distressing as it is sometimes we may need to see evidence that a person has passed away before we can really enter the grieving process proper.

It may be easier to liken bereavement to a physical injury. Loss causes a mental wound that requires time to heal and recover. The emotional response of grief helps to promote the healing and although the event or person remains in our memories forever, the raw pain and hurt at the shock of the initial loss recedes over time. In the next chapter we will look in more detail at these physical and emotional symptoms as well as some of the social and spiritual expressions of grief so that you can identify whether you are experiencing some of them in your own bereavement. These will all eventually subside as you navigate through the grief process.

Chapter 2 – The Symptoms Of Grief

We have mentioned that it is important to understand that grief affects people in different ways and to different degrees. No one person grieves in the same way since human beings are all unique and will react differently to different events. Your reaction to loss is governed to a large extent by the relationship you had with the person you have lost and by your personality and your own life experiences. How you express grief is in part shaped by your upbringing, expected social etiquette, religion and the cultural influences of your community. After a death, your symptoms of grieving may also be influenced by how you view death.

Nevertheless, there are common symptoms which although may appear frightening, are perfectly normal and are all part of the grieving process. The signs and symptoms of grief can broadly be divided into physical, emotional, social and spiritual in nature.

- **Physical** expressions of grief often include a multitude of reactions such as crying and/or sighing, headaches, frequent yawning, loss of appetite, difficulty sleeping, fatigue, restlessness, heart palpitations, aches and pains and muscular tension.

- **Emotional** expressions of grief include feelings of depression, sadness and intense yearning. But feelings of fear, anxiety, hopelessness, frustration, panic, anger, or guilt are also normal. For example, you may be angry at the doctor for their perceived failings in saving your loved one be angry at God for allowing an accident of nature to take your loved one away. You may feel intense guilt and blame yourself following a suicide and regret things that you may or may not have said before their loss. These are some of the most common emotional symptoms of bereavement.

- **Social** expressions of grief may include feelings of isolation and aloneness, inability to engage in any meaningful conversation and preferring your own company. If you normally enjoy company you may suddenly feel detached and cut off from the world and show limited or no interest in those around you.

- **Spiritual** or religious expressions of grief may include challenging your faith or beliefs and questioning the reason for your loss and suffering, challenging the purpose of life and the meaning of death.

Other symptoms of grief may include forgetfulness, trouble focusing and constantly changing your mind and being unable to make a firm decision. Rest assured that all these symptoms are normal adaptive reactions within the grieving process.

Please try not to make any major life-changing decisions if you can, for at least a year after your loss as you may not be in the right frame of mind to make a decision that can have a huge impact on the rest of your life. If you really need to, consider discussing your options with someone you are able to trust such as a close friend or seek professional advice.

Chapter 3 – The Different Stages Of Grief

The symptoms of grief we looked at in the last section are exhibited to varying degrees in the different phases of the grieving process as identified by Elisabeth Kübler-Ross in 1969 in her book 'On Death and Dying'. She identified a cycle of 5 emotional states or stages that naturally occur in our emotional responses after loss and change. She named these five stages of grief as denial, anger, bargaining, depression and acceptance.

They form a model to help us frame and identify what we may be feeling and better equip us to handle life and loss. At times people in grief may report additional stages but just remember that the process of grief is as unique as you are. It is important to know that the stages should be viewed loosely as there is no smooth transition from one stage to the next. Some people may not necessarily experience each stage; they may progress in non-linear order or even oscillate back and forth between stages. We may then ask why discuss the stages at all? The reason that it is useful is that it offers us a guideline as to what we can typically expect.

1. **SHOCK & DENIAL**- This is the first stage in the model and helps us survive the loss. You will most probably react to hearing of the loss with shock, numbness and disbelief, particularly if the death was sudden or unexpected. Shock and denial are defensive mechanisms in that they actually help us to cope and make survival possible. It is nature's way of allowing us only to handle as much as we are able to cope with. The individual may seek to spend some time alone in order to process the news. This stage may last for several weeks or months.

2. **ANGER & GUILT**–In this stage there may be a period of extreme anger where you may vent your anger at another person or object. However, unpleasant as it is, it is a necessary stage of the healing process. The angrier you feel, the more it will start to dissolve and the faster the healing. You may feel anger at the doctor for failing to save your loved one's life, direct your anger at another person who you feel was rightly or wrongly responsible or a relative who you felt was never around to help you or even take your anger out at God. Underlying the anger is pain and guilt, for

example you may feel guilt or remorse over things you did or didn't say or do before their death. Life feels chaotic and scary during this phase and anger is just an indicator of the depth of your love. The more you feel your anger, the more it will begin to dissolve and the quicker you will start the journey in healing.

3. **BARGAINING**- After a loss you may find yourself bargaining or negotiating with an imaginary force. For example you may ask 'Why me?" or "What if....?" You may also try to bargain with the upper powers for a way to bring the deceased back and reverse the loss. For example "I will never lose my temper again with him if you just bring him back". After a loss, bargaining may also take the form of a temporary pact. "What if I spent the rest of my life to help others". Then perhaps the loss can somehow be reversed. We want to turn the clock back to before the loss. Underlying this stage there is also the feeling of guilt as we may blame ourselves. The feelings and inner bargaining thoughts can last for minutes, weeks or months as we oscillate between different

stages.

4. **DEPRESSION, REFLECTION, LONELINESS**- After bargaining there may follow a long period of somber reflection and depression. You may wish to seek time to yourself in order to reflect on the memories you spent with your lost one. During this time, you begin to realize the true extent of your loss and that your loved one will never be coming back. You may experience feelings of emptiness or despair and these feelings seem like they will never lift. We should understand that this period of depression is not a sign that we are mentally ill but that it is an entirely appropriate reaction to an acute loss. Depression after a loss is often viewed as an aberration rather than a norm: a state that we need to be talked out of by well-intentioned friends and relatives. However this is an entirely normal stage of grief and encouragement to 'snap out of it' from others is not helpful during this period. To not experience any depression after the passing of a loved one would, in fact, be considered as highly unusual. If grief is a process of healing, then depression is one of the steps along the path to

recovery and rebuilding your life. As you start to adjust to life without your dear one, your life becomes a little calmer and more peaceful. Your physical symptoms alleviate, and your depression begins to recede.

5. **ACCEPTANCE & HOPE-** During this, the last of the stages in this grief model, you learn to accept and deal with the reality of your situation. Arriving at this stage may take a long time. We begin to live and feel present again, but we cannot do so until we have given grief its time. It may be helpful to you to know that most people who have suffered a devastating loss may never truly recover but over time the loss becomes part of that person's life such that the memories of the loved one no longer become all-consuming and disabling. There is a new permanent 'norm' and we adapt and reconstruct a life without the loved one in it but never forget them. We may have to re-assign roles or take on the duties that were previously performed by the loved one. The healing journey may simply just be experiencing more good days compared to bad ones as we accept the loss, start to rebuild our lives and make new social

connections. There may be periods when the acute pain resurfaces, this is common and does not mean we are back at square one in the healing process. You may find that these feelings occur around the time of significant events such as birthdays and anniversaries and will fade as the years pass.

Chapter 4 – Strategies For Coping

As we discussed grief is a very personal experience and unique to each individual. We have seen that the stages of grief can be non-linear and there may be periods of calmness interjected by periods of overwhelming emotions when a sudden event or comment triggers memories of the loved one This section provides some helpful strategies for coping with grief.

- **Talking about the loss** – Painful feelings and thoughts should not be bottled up as they serve to fuel the wounds. For real healing it is necessary to face your grief and actively deal with it. The pain needs to come out for you to start to heal. When friends or family ask how they can help, ask them to just be there for you and listen. It is important to express your thoughts and feelings. Try to expand your social network or invite a friend to lunch as this hastens the healing proces but beware of talking to some people whom you don't feel understand you as this may not be helpful.

- **Crying** – Just as you may need to talk about your loss you may also need to find an outlet for suppressed emotions so let the tears flow as this provides a way to release the stress hormones and toxins from the body. Crying also lowers blood pressure and reduces manganese, a mineral which directly affects our mood. Although it is well-known that women cry on average far more than men it is an accepted natural and healthy way to reduce emotional stress for all human beings so if you ever feel like crying please just go ahead and allow the pent-up emotions to come out.

- **Allow yourself the time to grief and feel sad** – in many ways the experience of grief is not dissimilar to recovering from a serious illnes. Time allows wounds to heal and repair. The recovery may take some time, don't put pressure on yourself to have to meet deadlines or commitments that you had made as people will understand. However, it is important that you do not stay passive for too long as research has shown that people who were more prone to focusing inwards and not actively trying to lift their mood (by talking to others or taking up a more active life) were more prone to still be depressed six months later.

- **Join a support group** – Some people find it helpful to join a general support group where you can share experiences with people who have gone through similar losses and therefore can derive comfort and support from each other. This can be a very effective way to promote healing and allows members to talk about their emotions and release their feelings in a safe, supportive, non-judgmental environment. Extremely traumatic losses, such as loss of a child or a suicide generally are better served in groups where all members share the same type of loss. Support groups may also introduce new friendships into your life, particularly if you find that your family members or regular friends are not able to offer you the necessary support or understanding. There may also be specialist therapeutic groups in your area where a psychologist or other professional facilitates the group with structured content. Each session focues on a specific theme to help people address a particular aspect of the grieving experience. For example, trouble sleeping, flashbacks or managing a particular emotional issue.

- **Stay active** – Try and stay active as much as you can, like walking the dog or undertaking new activities. Perhaps volunteer at a local charity or community centre, this will widen your social network and help you to focus on other people despite your own pain. Other activities might include reading a good book, seeing a movie with a friend, going on a trip, playing golf, arranging flowers or simply resuming other activities that you enjoyed doing before your loss. The goal is to try and keep yourself occupied with positive energy. All these activities help in quickening the recovery process and lessening the pain of the loss. Never feel guilty that you are somehow betraying the person you lost as they would not have wished to see you in mourning for the rest of your life.

- **Remembering your loved one's memory** – Anniversaries, birthdays and other occassions that remind you of your loved one can be particularly stressful. Chat to family and friends about it as they may have suggestions, or consider introducing new traditions to mark special occasions. You might also wish to compile a photo album or plant a tree or bench in memory of your loved one. If your loved one had a cause, foundation or charity then you might think about continuing the cause in some capacity to honor their memory.

- **Express yourself creatively -** You might also think about writing or blogging which is a very good activity to express yourself creatively. Simply writing a letter or email, even if you never send it, can be incredibly powerful and allow you to release your emotions and bring clarity to the pain you are going through. Other creative outlets include painting and even baking a cake which all help you to relax and increases a sense of conrol.

- **Avoid using chemicals to dull your feelings -** Trying to suppress your feelings by consuming alcohol or taking illicit drugs has the effect of causing a person to stay depressed for much longer and eventually, one way or another, you must come to terms with your grief.

- **Take care of your physical health** – Eat healthily and get enough sleep. Grief takes enormous physical as well as emotional energy. Rest, exercise and eating properly are essential to healing. If you are having difficulties digesting then try to eat smaller portions of healthy foods with plenty of fibre rather than large meals. You should also try to avoid processed foods as this can cause you to become irritable and suffer fatigue and mood swings. If you have trouble sleeping, take small naps or try to relax by listening to some music. Getting a massage can also be incredibly relaxing and reduce blood pressure.

- **Get a pet** – If you like animals getting a pet to take care of can help you lift the depression, reduce stress and allow you take your mind off your loss. It is particularly beneficial for those grieving the break up of a marriage or a separation since taking care of a pet, particularly a dog, requires a routine and forces you to be active. The interaction and love given and received from a dog or cat can be incredibly therapeutic in the healing process. The act of stroking a pet, in similar fashion to cuddling a loved one, increases the level of oxytocin (often called the "feel good" chemical) in the brain. It also diffuses stress as the heart rate slows down and the body's natural chemicals (cortisol and adrenaline) switch off.

- **Seek professional help** – A therapist can help with tools and techniques to support you and help you come to terms with your loss. Grief counsellors can offer a safe and confidential space to explore, talk about and make sense of your feelings in a non-judgmental way. They may use cognitive behavior therapy or other techniques to support you through bereavement either on a short or long-term basis, through this difficult time. Your doctor may also have recommendations of therapists who specialize in this field that they might be able to refer you to.

Chapter 5 – What Happens If There Is No Improvement?

There is no specific timetable for the process of healing. Everyone is different and it cannot be overstated that the experience and symptoms of physical and emotional stress is unique for each person and for each loss. The timing and order of the healing process will also differ for each individual.

- Accepting the reality of the loss
- Permitting yourself to experience the pain
- Learning to accept and deal with the reality of the loss
- Making plans for the future and developing new relationships and friendships

These differences are normal and most people adapt to the loss after 6 months. Gradually the feelings lessen, and it's possible to accept loss and start to move forward in life. The grief changes from an all-consuming sadness to an integrated form in which the sadness and yearning are much more subdued.

For some people however, the feeling of loss persists or even intensifies, and there is no improvement. There is still

- A persistent longing for the deceased person
- A general sense of purposelessness
- Continued difficulty accepting the loss
- Anger at the death
- Difficulty taking up new activities or resuming day to day routines

If this happens you may have complicated grief or prolonged grief disorder (PGD). Around 10% of grieving people experience complicated grief. If so please seek professional help as soon as you can from a specialist who has experience in complicated grief as it is a serious disorder that impedes the acceptance process essential for moving forward. 4% of individuals who have this disorder go on to take their own life. Medical research has found that targeted cognitive behavioural therapy (CBT) can be effective in treating PGD. The approach may involve revisiting and talking about the deceased, working through the emotions and developing strategies for coping.

The most important aspect of grief is not to let it paralyze your life and stop you from ever living again and finding peace. It is important to take the steps to move through it so that you can once again find happiness.

Chapter 6 – Helping Someone Else Who Is Grieving

We have looked at the symptoms and process of grieving and various tools to aid in the recovery process but what happens if someone we care about is grieving. Well the tools and techniques we looked at can also be applied to help you support a grieving family member or friend. Rather than being too worried about what to say or do for someone who is grieving or concerned that you might say the wrong thing you can instead provide them with your time and support. This can include:

- **Offering a listening ear** – Rather than talking and being worried you might say the wrong thing it is more important to listen to them in a compassionate and empathic way. Never force someone to talk if they don't feel comfortable to but let them know that you are there to listen to them. You will find that more often than not, the bereaved person finds benefit when their loss is acknowledged. You should keep the talking to the minimum and some suggestions you could make include:

- "Do you feel like talking?"
- "I am not sure what to say but I want you to know that I care."
- "Tell me what I can do."

If you can't think of what to say, even sitting in silence and squeezing their hand or giving them a comforting hug can be enough.

Be aware that some statements may not be helpful though, so please avoid saying:

- "You should move on with your life…"
- "He/she is in a better place"
- " It is fate and God's will"

- **Offering practical assistance** – When a person is griefing they may find it difficult to ask for help. You can offer them practical support such as helping with funeral arrangements during the early stages, doing the shopping or other errand, helping with household chores or childcare support or accompany them somewhere. Rather than simply saying "What can I do for you?" you could instead be more specific and say "I am going to the shops later, can I get you anything?"

- **Providing them with ongoing support** – We have seen that the grieving process varies considerably for each person and some recover faster than others. Be aware that your grieving friend or family member may need your ongoing support for a long time after the death. Stay in regular contact with them, drop by and send messages or cards to let them know that you are thinking of them. It is well-known that receiving cards or messages with a few kind words can help someone who is depressed or low to recover and heal much faster.

- **Giving them the time to heal** – The healing process cannot be hurried and may take months or even years so give them the time to heal. Stay patient, don't get impatient or agitated that you are not gaining any fun or benefit at the moment from the relationship. A good friend or family member will be there for each other through good times and bad.

- **Being alert to signs of complicated grief** – In the last chapter we looked at grief which does not appear to be improving even after a considerable time. If you believe this applies to your friend then this may well be a sign that the person is suffering from prolonged grief disorder. Here, you may need to encourage them to seek professional help, particularly if there are warning signs such as alcohol or drug abuse or talking about dying or suicide. It may be difficult to raise your concerns but you could try saying to them "I am worried (that you aren't eating or sleeping) – perhaps you should look into getting professional help". You may know a therapist and help to set up an appointment for them. Seeking professional help right away is important as left untreated, complicated grief can lead to life-changing health issues, clinical depression and even suicide.

Conclusion

We grieve for many different reasons and we all grief in different ways. There are no right or wrong ways of experiencing grief although some thoughts and actions after suffering a loss can be more helpful than others.

However, whether we are grieving because we have lost a loved one or grieving the dissolution of a marriage or close friendship there are ways that we can hasten the healing process. Maintaining a strong social support network, undertaking physical activities, developing new routines, taking up creative hobbies, permitting yourself the time to grief, being compassionate to yourself, attending support groups and seeing a professional grief specialist can all help with the emotional and physical symptoms of grief.

There may be times when we feel we have moved forward in our lives but a sudden or unexpected event or a special occasion, piece of music or place may bring back memories of the loss and the grief comes surging back like a tidal wave. Revisit the coping strategies in the book at any time you feel the need to and remember that time is the greatest healer.

It may be helpful to consider that the best way we can respect the loss of a loved one is to live and fulfill the lives that they would have wanted for us as they surely would not want us to spend the remainder of our lives in grieving. Rather they would have wanted us to let go of our pain and get back to finding happiness again as quickly as possible.

Thank you for downloading this book, I hope it was helpful for you during this most profoundly distressing time. Please leave a review for this book on Amazon.com using the following links as I would like to hear your comments and feedback.

https://www.amazon.co.uk/dp/B074G4HVBL

https://www.amazon.com/dp/B074G4HVBL

Printed in Great Britain
by Amazon